Glass Making Using Microwave Kiln Simplified For Beginners

Complete Picture Step By Step Guide On How To Make Your Own Fused Glass Jewelry and Pendant via Microwave Kiln with Ease at the Comfort of your Home

Petrina Purser

TABLE OF CONTENTS

INTRODUCTION 4

CHAPTER ONE 6

   FUNDAMENTAL ITEMS YOU NEED 6

CHAPTER 2 12

   PREPARING YOUR KILN PAPER 12

CHAPTER 3 14

   CUTTING AND BREAKING THE GLASS 14

CHAPTER 4 19

   PUTTING YOUR GLASS IN THE KILN 19

CHAPTER 5 22

   HEATING UP THE KILN 22

CHAPTER 6 26

   REMOVING IT FROM THE MICROWAVE . 26

CHAPTER 7 29

   PUTTING FINISHING TOUCHES 29

CHAPTER 8 30

   TRIM IT INTO A PIECE OF JEWELRIES 30

CHAPTER 9 32

   COMPLETED PIECES 32

THE END 35

INTRODUCTION

Making glass gems is fun and will show you the standards of glass combining. With training, you ought to have the option to accomplish predictable outcomes in microwave terminating. You will require a microwave oven, which is a little fired fiber holder that fits inside the microwave. The microwave furnace catches microwave energy and gathers it in the terminating chamber. The idea is like utilizing an amplifying glass to center daylight.

It is hard to accept that the microwaves we use to warm soup and heat potatoes can get adequately hot to circuit or soften glass. In actuality, not exclusively can microwaves meld glass, yet most stoves can do it in under 10 min.

The greatest test to microwave terminating is the quick warming rate. A microwave oven arrives at 1,650°F (899°C) in just 5-10 min. Terminating times rely upon the wattage of the microwave; the lower the wattage, the more drawn out the terminating time. Nonetheless, firings can be controlled to accomplish steady outcomes.

Just little glass tasks can withstand fast warming. The glass ought to be no bigger than 1 x 1½ in. what's more, no thicker than two layers of 1/8-in. stained glass. The glass should be perfect; even an oily unique mark can make the glass split up during the underlying warming.

CHAPTER ONE

FUNDAMENTAL ITEMS YOU NEED

you are working with glass and extremely hot temperatures. Security is an unquestionable requirement. Security for your eyes, lungs, and skin is of most extreme significance. Along these lines, don't take alternate routes. Simply don't !!!

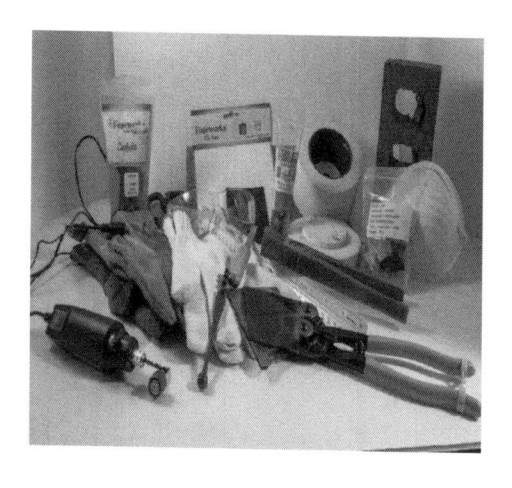

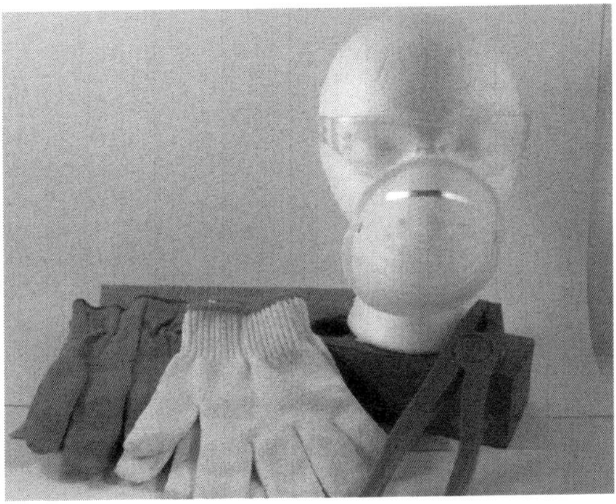

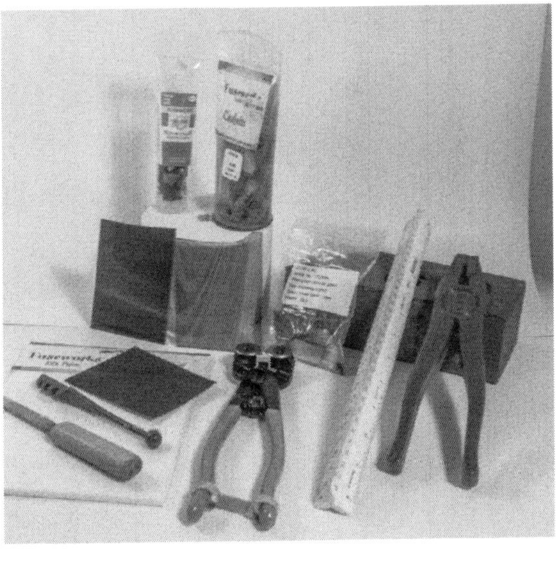

Strong gloves will ensure your hands when breaking the glass.

Warmth Proof Gloves-They are for taking care of the furnace subsequent to terminating and the end result after eliminating the piece from the oven.

Glass Pliers - For breaking glass.

Residue Mask - So you don't get glass in your mouth, nose and lungs

Wellbeing Glasses - For breaking glass and use with the drill to complete your undertaking.

A Heat safe surface - To sit the furnace on after the terminating interaction. Being a cheapo, I went to the tool shop and purchased a block. It turns out great.

A portion of the things you should have are:

THE KILN (clearly)

Oven Paper

A glass shaper

A Straight Edge

A File

Glass Pliers

A few things you should add later

Various kinds of glass

Glass/Tile Nippers

Sandpaper

Drill, (for example, a Dremel) .

CHAPTER 2

PREPARING YOUR KILN PAPER

Furnace (Kiln) paper ought to be laid on the bed of the oven each time you use it. The fuse works paper I use, I can get four firings from each sheet. Sheet are 5/8" X 5/8". Just cut it into quarters when you get a piece of paper out of the bundle.

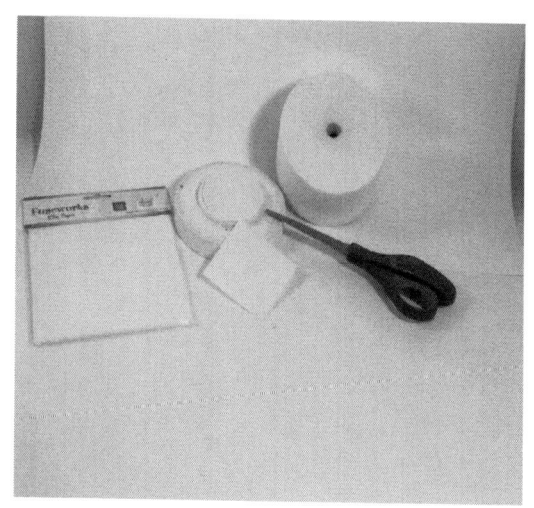

I for one decide to manage the paper into a roundabout example close in size to the raised foundation of the furnace. That gives me a thought of the territory I need to work with.

Additionally, ensure that the glass doesn't contact the side of the furnace. It will stick and can harm your oven.

This paper is a one hit wonder. Furnace paper can't be reused. One use and throw it.

CHAPTER 3

CUTTING AND BREAKING THE GLASS

You won't slice totally through the glass, you are all the more scoring the glass. You are making a slight indention in the glass with the goal that you can see where the break will happen.

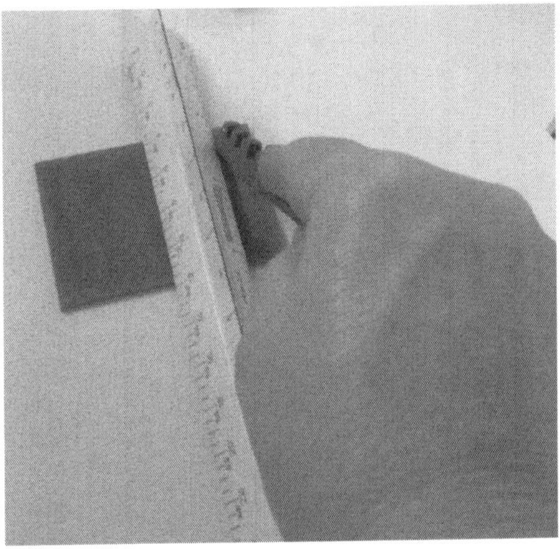

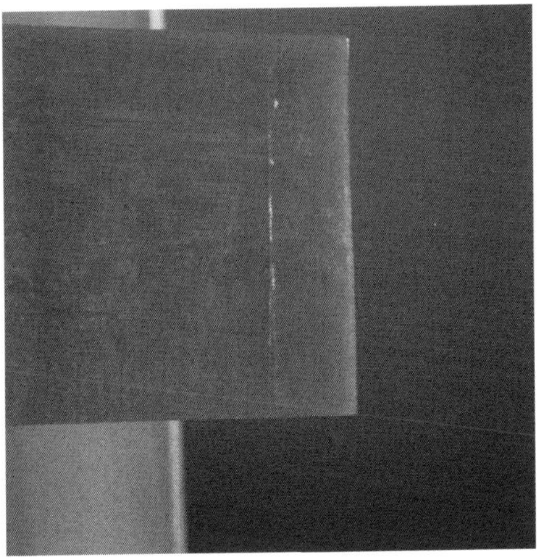

Assume your straightedge and position it on the glass. At that point you take the glass shaper and applying pressure, you go the length of the glass. This is will leave the score line as found in the last photograph.

This is the line that you will break.

Here is a touch of something that may be useful, you ought to hear the glass shaper coming the outside of the glass. On the off chance that you don't hear it, you likely need to apply more pressing factor.

I have utilized three unique strategies to break the glass. Two were very compelling, one not in any manner.

Strategy one..... Glass Pliers, they handle the glass solidly without gnawing into it. Incredible, this is the most ideal way.

Strategy two... Until I got glass pincers, I utilized the edge of my kitchen ledge. It functioned admirably.

Strategy three.... Utilizing customary family unit pincers. Don't, it will chomp into the glass.

After picking your strategy, simply snap it rapidly, much the same as ripping off a swathe, get it done.

CHAPTER 4

PUTTING YOUR GLASS IN THE KILN

Whenever you have cut and broken the glass, the time has come to fabricate your creation. It is your task. It tends to be however many tones as you pick. Simply play with it, have a good time. Simply appreciate the experience of making.

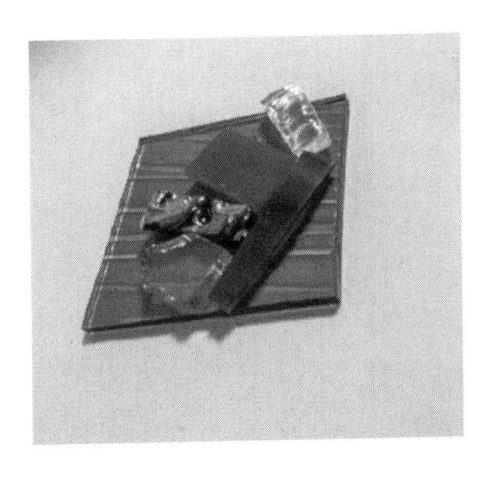

This is pretty much straightforward. Spot the furnace paper, place your plan on top and put the cover on. Indeed, ensure none of the glass is contacting the bed or the sides of the oven. It isn't that I have done it or anything, we should simply say I know now not. Likewise, on the off chance that you think something moved when you put the cover on, you can check it before you begin terminating. When you begin terminating, don't eliminate the cover until the terminating cycle is finished.

Simply know that in the event that you do eliminate the cover, you may need to realign the glass to get the impact you needed.

CHAPTER 5

HEATING UP THE KILN

When you put the furnace into the microwave, you should sort out the best an ideal opportunity for your microwave.

My microwave is 900 watts. Contingent upon the kind of glass I am combining, it as a rule fires in around 5 minutes to 5 minutes and 30 seconds.

Check the wattage on your microwave. It will fire quicker with a higher wattage.

When the oven is up to temperature, the middle opening in the highest point of the oven will shine, that is the point at which you will realize that the terminating is occurring. It is then that you eliminate the furnace from the microwave.

The piece needs to sit in the oven for 30 minutes whenever it is eliminated from the microwave. This is to permit time for the glass to solidify and meld. This can be an extremely boisterous interaction, so in the event that you hear something

that sound awful coming from inside the furnace, endure it, don't lift the cover until the full 30 minutes terminates. I normally go get another thing to do. I'm not patient. To a few of us, 30 minutes seems like until the end of time. In the event that you accomplish something different, your impression of time is adjusted and the time has passed before you know it.

Whenever you have taken out the cover from the oven and spot the highest point of the oven with the little opening down on a warmth safe surface, it needs to cool, it has held enough warmth to take a strong, separating it into a magma like puddle and permitted it to turn into a strong again so it needs to cool. Try not to utilize it again until it is cool to the

touch. Leave the base setting on the block. It is fine where it is.

CHAPTER 6

REMOVING IT FROM THE MICROWAVE

Don't under any condition grab hold of the furnace exposed gave. Extreme injury will most definitely happen. On the off chance that you are drawing near to the terminating to end, glove up. You should wear gloves when dealing with the furnace and the completed piece after it sets.

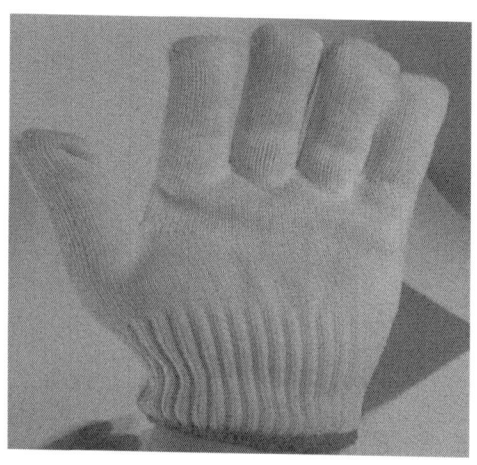

Note to the shrewd. Try not to clutch it for long, albeit these gloves make moving the oven tolerable. It can in any case harm the gloves on the off chance that you hold it excessively long. Same with the terminated piece that emerges from the oven. At the point when you move, move with goal. Move the oven to the warmth safe surface (recall my block). The equivalent applies to the completed piece. It is still hot.

At times, it doesn't warm equally and you can see it in the completed undertaking. You have two options here, figure out how to cherish the defects or you can attempt to fire it once more. Simply make sure to utilize new oven paper and now and then terminating the piece again functions admirably, in some cases it doesn't.

CHAPTER 7

PUTTING FINISHING TOUCHES

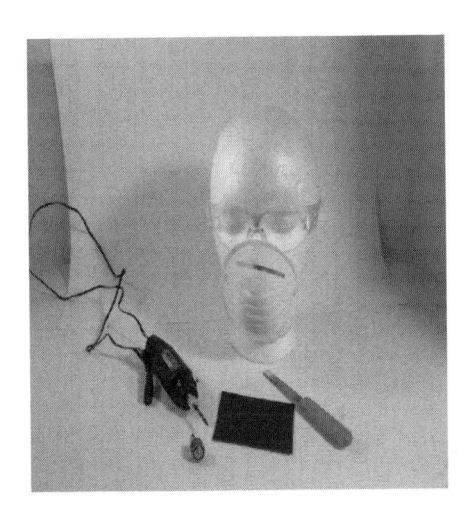

Utilize your record, sand paper or borer to smooth any harsh edges left This will make you piece a smooth completed, pleasantly cleaned pendant. Make sure to utilize wellbeing glass and your molecule veil.

CHAPTER 8

TRIM IT INTO A PIECE OF JEWELRIES

You can make a pendant, a ring, a wristband or a couple of stud. It is totally up to you. Make what you need, make what you love, simply make.

E6000 turns out extraordinary for following the completed piece to the clear or finding that you pick.

CHAPTER 9

COMPLETED PIECES

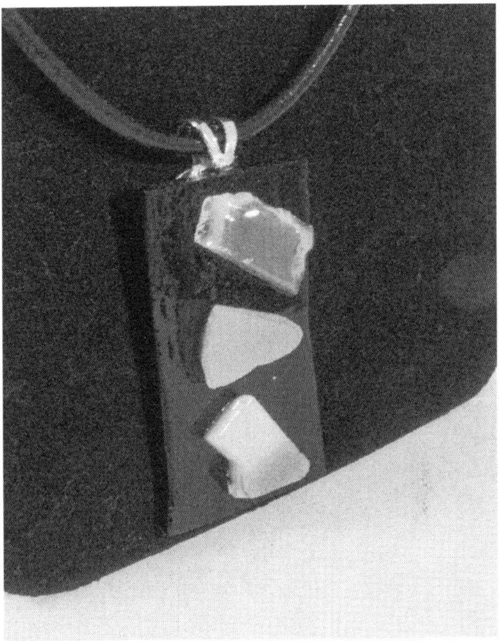

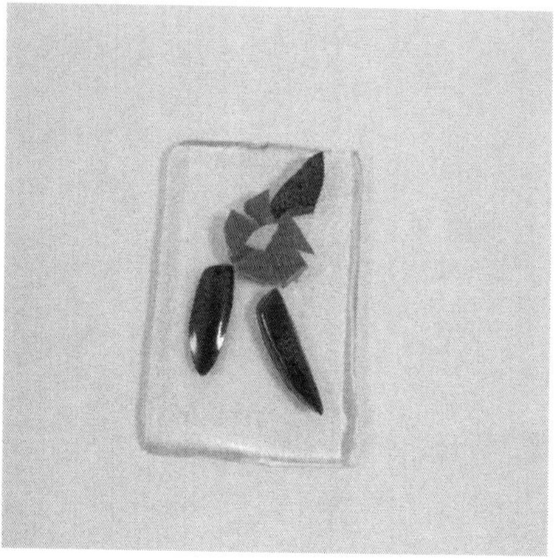

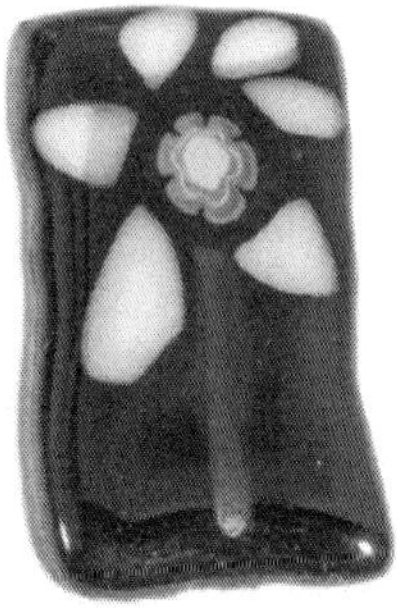

THE END

Made in the USA
Columbia, SC
15 December 2023